SQUARE

RECTANGLE

DIAMOND

TRIANGLE

HEXAGON

OVAL

CIRCLE

First Edition 1 2 3 4 5 6 7 8 9 10

Library of Congress Cataloging in Publication Data
McMillan, Bruce. Fire engine shapes / by Bruce McMillan.   p.   cm. Summary: Photographs of various parts of a fire engine depict different geometrical shapes. ISBN 0-688-07842-7; ISBN 0-688-07843-5 (lib. bdg.) : 1. Geometry—Juvenile literature. 2. Fire-engines—Juvenile literature. [1. Shape—Pictorial works. 2. Geometry—Pictorial works. 3. Fire engines—Pictorial works.] I. Title QA447.M395 1988 628.9'25—dc19 87-38145 CIP AC

FOR KYLE

S.P.F.D.

FIRE ENGINE SHAP

BY BRUCE McMILLAN

LOTHROP, LEE & SHEPARD BOOKS · NEW YORK

ENGINE 5

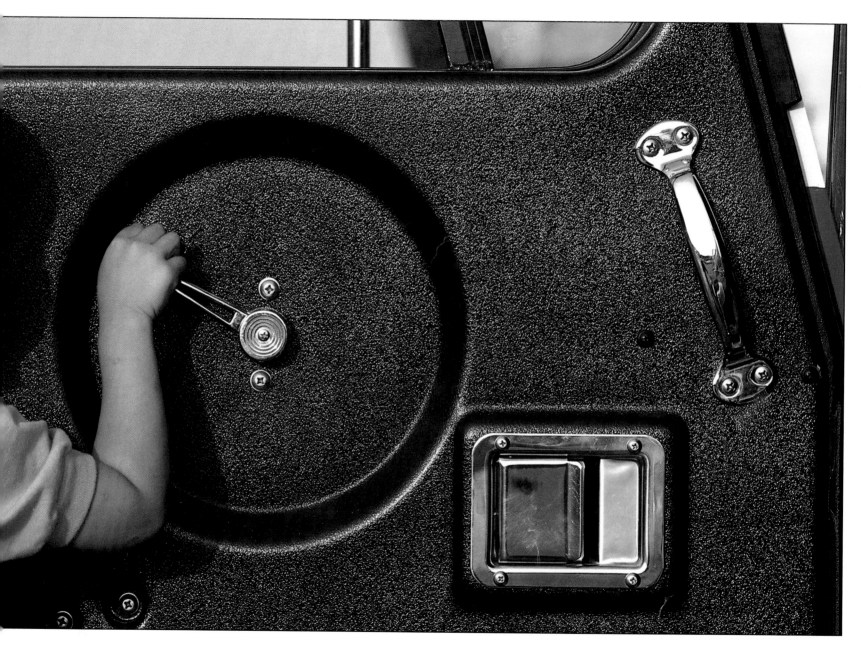

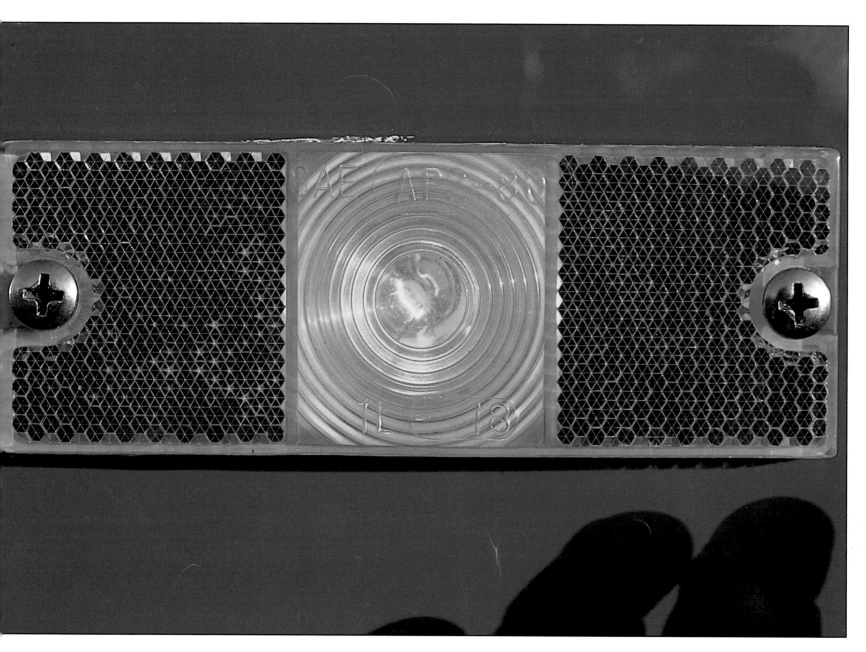

ENGINE 5

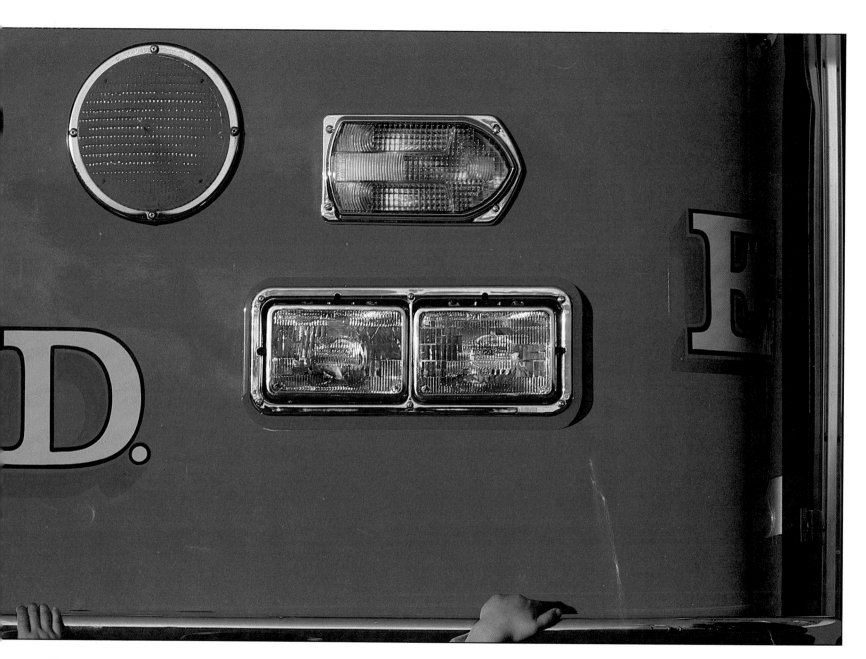

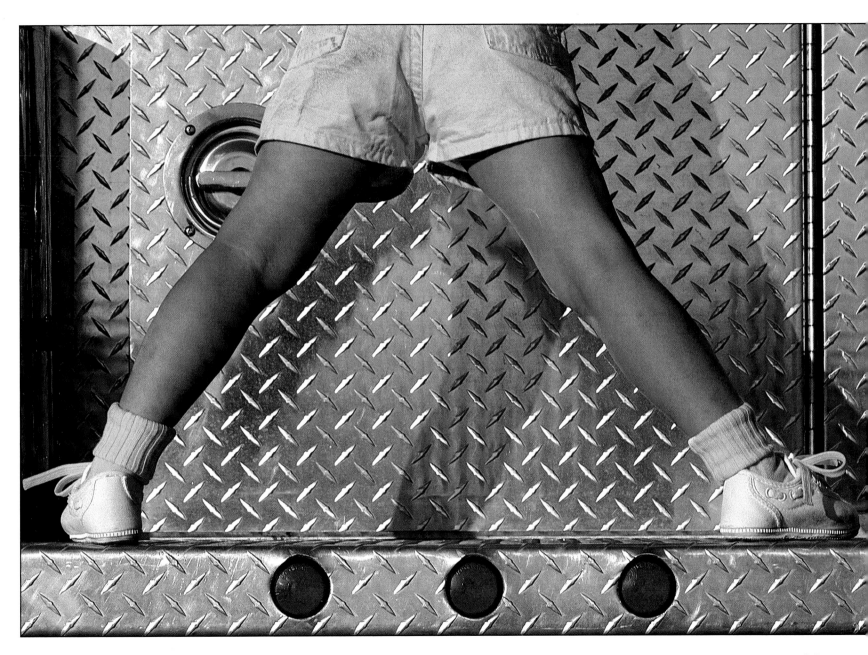

FOUR-YEAR-OLD STEPHANIE KAORI TAMAKI deserves special thanks for the role she played in the photography of this book. She was a joy to work with. Thanks also to Stephanie's parents, Atsushi "Atchan" Tamaki and Shinobu Tamaki, to Chief Philip McGouldrick, and to all the firefighters at Engine 5 Station.

Fire Engine Shapes was photographed at Engine 5 Station in South Portland, Maine. The fire engine is an Emergency One, with a totally encapsulated cab. It carries 1200 feet of 4-inch hose, 700 feet of 2½-inch hose, 700 feet of 1¾-inch hose, and 750 gallons of water, and can pump 1500 gallons per minute.

The photographs were taken using a Nikon FE2 with 24, 55 Micro, 105, or 200mm lens. The camera was tripod mounted for most shots. Lighting was late afternoon and early evening sunlight, balanced with a color-correcting blue filter. The lighting was primarily natural daylight, with reflected light or fill flash sometimes added. The film used was Kodachrome 64, processed by Kodak.

WHAT IS A SHAPE?
All objects have form, or shape. Universal shapes have been given specific names, which help us describe what we see around us. Each spread of this book contains a pair of photographs which feature the same dominant shape. Other shapes may also be found within each photograph. The index below lists seven universal shapes that can be found in the pictures.